扫描文章前的二维码
收听该故事的英文音频

"伟人的少年故事"丛书

创新的火花

—— 打破隔阂创造历史的伟人 ——

(斯里兰卡)努雷·维塔奇(Nury Vittachi) 著
斯泰帕·张(Step Cheung) 图
朱之翀 译　张 群 审校

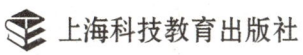

图书在版编目(CIP)数据

创新的火花：打破隔阂创造历史的伟人 /（斯里）努雷·维塔奇（Nury Vittachi）著；朱之翔译 .—上海：上海科技教育出版社，2018.8

（"伟人的少年故事"丛书）

书名原文：The Inventor's Spark

ISBN 978-7-5428-6703-2

I.①创… II.①努… ②朱… III.①科学家—生平事迹—世界—青少年读物 IV.① K816.1—49

中国版本图书馆 CIP 数据核字（2018）第 069075 号

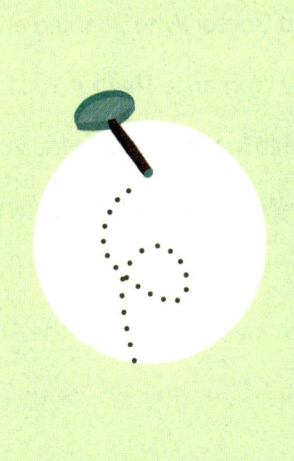

Contents

Karl Benz The Boy Who Combined a Bike and a Train to Invent the Car   2

John Walker The Failed Doctor Who Sparked an Idea   10

Mary The Alchemist The Woman to Thank if You Like Chocolate   19

Garrett Morgan The Man in the Burning House   26

Gregorio Zara The Boy Who Lost His Chance but Got It Back   35

Ada Byron Lovelace The Unloved Teenager and the Giant Calculator   43

Tu Youyou The Scientist and the Secret in the Ancient Book   51

Balamurali Ambati and Sho Timothy Yano The Impossibly Young Doctors   58

Blaise Pascal The Motherless Child Who Solved His Father's Problem   64

Rachel Carson The Girl Torn Between Two Careers   72

目 录

卡尔·本茨　发明汽车的男孩　2

约翰·沃克　灵光闪现的"失败"医生　10

炼金术士玛丽　巧克力爱好者感谢的女子　19

加勒特·摩根　着火房屋里的男子　26

格雷戈里奥·扎拉　机会失而复得的男孩　35

阿达·拜伦·洛夫莱斯　缺爱少女和大型计算器　43

屠呦呦　发现古籍秘密的科学家　51

艾姆巴蒂和矢野祥　令人难以置信的年轻医生　58

布莱斯·帕斯卡　帮助父亲解决难题的失恃男孩　64

蕾切尔·卡森　在两种职业之间摇摆的女孩　72

THE BOY WHO COMBINED A BIKE AND A TRAIN TO INVENT THE CAR

卡尔·本茨
发明汽车的男孩

LITTLE KARL REMEMBERED almost nothing about his father. The boy was only two years old when the man died.

But his mother Josephine spoke about him.

"Your father was a train driver," she said. And she would show him the big, powerful, steaming **locomotive**[1] trains that existed in those days.

Karl and his mother had a hard life. They had no money. But she **instilled**[2] values in him, and encouraged him to study hard and be ambitious.

Karl Benz, who was born in 1844 in Germany, did so well in his studies that when he was nine, he was sent to a science school called the Lyceum. From there, while still in his early teens, he studied at the **poly technical**[3] University.

In those days, there were no planes or cars, and rich people travelled in horse-drawn carriages.

Poor people like Karl would just walk, or, if they were lucky, they would ride bicycles.

One day, while riding his cheap old bicycle to school, he had a thought. What if you could build an engine, something like existed in one of his father's trains, but really, really small — so small, that you could put it into a carriage or even onto a bicycle.

年幼的卡尔对于父亲几乎没有什么记忆。在他两岁的时候,父亲就去世了。

但母亲约瑟芬经常提起他的父亲。

"你的父亲是一位火车司机,"约瑟芬说。她带卡尔去看他们那个时代里那些体积巨大、动力强劲的蒸汽火车。

卡尔和母亲生活得很艰难。他们没有钱,但约瑟芬向卡尔灌输着正确的价值观,并鼓励他努力学习、志存高远。

卡尔·本茨(Karl Benz)1844年出生在德国。他的学习成绩非常好,因此在9岁时,他被送到了一所叫作"学园"(Lyceum,吕克昂,古希腊哲学家亚里士多德在雅典讲学之地名)的理科学校。所以说,在青少年时代早期,他就进入大学深造了。

那时没有飞机,也没有汽车,富人们坐着马车旅行。

而像卡尔这样的穷人只能走路,如果他们运气好,可以骑骑自行车。

有一天,当卡尔骑着他那辆廉价的旧自行车去学校时,突然灵光一闪:如果能够发明一种发动机,像他父亲开的火车里的那种发动机一样,但却比它小很多——小到能够放进一辆马车或是一辆自行车里,会发生什么呢?

① **locomotive** [ˌləʊkə'məʊtɪv] *adj.* 火车头的,运动的、移动的;*n.* 机车、火车头
② **instill** [ɪn'stɪl] *vt.* 逐渐灌输
③ **polytechnical** [ˌpɒli'teknɪkəl] *adj.* 多工艺的(等于 polytechnic);*n.* 工艺学校

It would be like a tiny little, one-person train — a horseless carriage!

Although he was training to be a locksmith, he decided to change course and study locomotive engineering, and follow the steps of his much-missed father.

At the age of 15, Karl managed to get into a big university to study mechanical engineering, and afterwards worked as an engineer for various companies.

But he was still thinking about his mini-engine idea, and when he was 28, he started to become more **entrepreneurial**①.

Encouraged by his new wife, a lively girl called Bertha, he invented different **mechanisms**②, such as an **ignition**③ system, **spark plugs**④, a **gear shift**⑤ and all sorts of things that you would need to have in the "horseless carriage" of his dreams.

When he found a friend who ran a bicycle repair shop, everything came together. Using **wire wheels**⑥ from bicycles and other elements from the engines he had invented, the first car was born: The Benz Patent Motorwagen.

It looked like a big tricycle, but it moved by itself just fine, and could take you up and down the street. You didn't need a horse, and you didn't have to pedal! It was **astonishing**⑦.

那可能就会创造出一辆小型的单人火车——不用马拉的马车!

卡尔之前接受的训练是成为一名锁匠,所以他决定改变自己所学的课程,去追随他思念已久的父亲的脚步,研习机车工程学。

15岁时,卡尔成功地考入了一所大学,研习机械工程专业。毕业后,他成了一名工程师,为不同的公司工作。

但他仍然不时想起那个小型发动机的创意。28岁时,他开始创业。

在他的妻子——一个名叫贝莎的活泼女孩的鼓励下,他发明了许多不同的机械装置,比如点火装置、火花塞、变速杆,以及其他所有他梦想的"不用马拉的马车"所需的配件。

当他与一位经营自行车修理店的男子成为朋友后,一切都变得顺利起来。将自行车的辐条式车轮和卡尔发明的发动机所用配件组装起来,世界上第一辆汽车诞生了:奔驰专利一号汽车。

这辆汽车看起来像是一辆大型的自行车,但行驶的速度很快,能够在大街小巷中穿梭。你不需要马匹去拉动它,也不需要像骑自行车那样蹬它!太令人惊讶了!

---

① **entrepreneurial** [ˌɒntrəprə'nɜːrɪəl; -'njʊərɪ-] *adj.* 企业家的、创业者的,中间商的
② **mechanism** ['mek(ə)nɪz(ə)m] *n.* 机制、原理、途径、进程,机械装置、技巧
③ **ignition** [ɪg'nɪʃ(ə)n] *n.* 点火、点燃、着火、燃烧,点火开关、点火装置
④ **spark plug**: *n.* [电][机]火花塞,带头人、中坚分子
⑤ **gear shift** 换挡装置,变速杆
⑥ **wire wheel** 辐条式车轮
⑦ **astonish** [ə'stɒnɪʃ] *v.* 使……惊讶、使……诧异

Karl's wife Bertha believed that it could do more than go up and down the street to amazed looks: it could take people long distances. So, without telling him, she borrowed it and took their children with her — using his machine to drive out of the city to visit **relatives**[①].

The trip was a great success — and the age of cars had begun.

If Karl Benz's train-driving father was looking down from heaven, he would surely be proud of his son, the inventor of the car.

卡尔的妻子贝莎相信,这种汽车的功能不只限于在街上行驶、使路人瞠目结舌而已,人们还能驾驶着它长途旅行。所以她在没有告诉卡尔的情况下,独自带着孩子们开车出城,拜访亲戚去了。

这次旅行很成功——汽车时代来临了。

如果卡尔那位曾是火车司机的父亲从天堂往下看,一定会为他的儿子——汽车发明者——而感到骄傲吧!

① relative ['relətɪv],美 ['rɛlətɪv] n. 亲戚

THE FAILED DOCTOR WHO SPARKED AN IDEA

约翰·沃克
灵光闪现的"失败"医生

YOUNG JOHN WALKER PROBABLY felt like a failure.

He was given a job as an assistant to a **surgeon**① at the age of 15. His parents hoped he would become a doctor himself.

But he hated most things about it: the illnesses and the unhappy people, and the difficulty of knowing whether you were helping or harming people.

So he gave up the profession.

Instead, he made a quiet job for himself doing the one part that he did like. He became a chemist, mixing medicines and selling them from a small shop in the UK. This was in the early 1800s.

One day, he became intrigued by a puzzle. There were so many things you could make instantly — you could turn **powder**② into drinks, or sand into **cement**③. Was there a way to instantly make fire?

Fire is such an important and useful thing that humans had been dealing with this question for a long time. More than a million years ago, a type of early man called **Homo erectus**④ was making fire the old way, rubbing sticks together, or making sparks by smashing pieces of a rock called **flint**⑤ together. Modern humans, **Homo sapiens**⑥, often still used the same method, generating sparks to light things.

青年约翰·沃克（John Walker）的人生不太成功。

当他 15 岁时，他得到了一份外科医生助手的工作。他的父母希望他成为一位医生。

但约翰讨厌与医学相关的大部分事物：疾病、心情沮丧的人们以及治疗所遇到的难题——医生无法判断自己是在帮助患者还是在伤害患者。

所以他放弃了这份职业。

取而代之的是，约翰选择了一份自己喜欢的安静的工作。那时是 19 世纪早期，他成了一名药剂师，并在英国开了一家小店，销售自己研制的药剂。

有一天，他突然对一个问题产生了兴趣：世界上有那么多可以迅速生产出来的东西——用粉末可以迅速调制饮品，用沙石可以迅速生产水泥。有没有一种快速生火的方法呢？

长期以来，人们都在想办法解决生火的难题，因为火在生活中实在是太重要、太有用了。100 多万年前，早期的人类——直立人通过摩擦树枝或撞击一种叫打火石的石块来生火，而现代人类——智人仍然在用同样的方法生火照明。

① **surgeon** ['sɜːdʒ(ə)n] *n.* 外科医生
② **powder** ['paʊdə] *n.* 粉、粉末、［化工］［军］火药、尘土；*vt.* 使成粉末、撒粉、搽粉；*vi.* 搽粉、变成粉末
③ **cement** [sɪ'ment] *n.* 水泥、接合剂
④ **Homo erectus** 直立人
⑤ **flint** [flɪnt] *n.* 燧石、打火石、极硬的东西
⑥ *Homo sapiens* 智人

Making fire took a long time, which was tiring, and did not always work.

In China, around the year AD 950, a man had the idea of **soaking**① little **sticks**② with chemicals that made them flammable.

If you wanted to light a fire quickly, you could get some flints and try to make sparks which would set the little "fire inch sticks" alight.

It made the process slightly quicker, but not much. You still had to spend a long time trying to create sparks.

By the 1800s, people in Europe were trying to find quicker ways of making fire. Some carried chemical sticks plus a bottle of a dangerous chemical to dip them in, which would cause them to burst into flames.

In another method, chemicals were wrapped in a glass bubble which was wrapped in paper and you had to **smash**③ it (some people did it with their teeth) to get the chemicals to mix and burn.

All the methods were **tricky**④, inconvenient and dangerous.

但这种生火方式耗时很长，人们常常因此疲惫不堪，而且还经常不成功。

❦

公元 950 年左右，中国的一名男子想出了一个主意，他将小棍子浸没在某种特定的化学品中，从而使它们变得易燃。

如果你想要快速生火，你可以敲击打火石，产生火星将这些"打火棍"点燃。

这种方式加速了生火的进程，但还不够快。人们还是需要花很长时间去生火。

19 世纪时，欧洲人尝试找到快速生火的方法。有人将沾有化学品的小棍子浸泡在另一种危险的化学品中，从而使小棍子可以一下子燃烧起来。

还有一种方法是，将一些特定的化学品用纸张包裹后存放在玻璃泡中。想要生火时，人们打碎玻璃泡（有些人用牙齿咬），取出化学品，混合后它们就会燃烧起来。

所有的方法实行起来都很困难，并且很危险。

---

① **soak** [səʊk] vt. 吸收、吸入、沉浸在（工作或学习中）、使……上下湿透；vi. 浸泡、渗透
② **stick** [stɪk] vt. 刺、戳、伸出、粘贴；vi. 坚持、伸出、粘住；n. 棍、手杖
③ **smash** [smæʃ] vt. 粉碎、使破产、溃裂；n. 破碎、扣球、冲突、大败；vi. 粉碎、打碎
④ **tricky** ['trɪkɪ] adj. 狡猾的、机警的 [trickier, trickiest]

John Walker tried to mix chemicals together too, to see what would happened. One day, he got a **blob**① of something very sticky on the end of a long stick. He scraped it along his stone floor to try to get the blob off.

Instead, it burst into flames.

John Walker had invented the first convenient **match**②. All you had to do was scrape it along a rough surface and it would instantly change from being a cold, dry stick of wood to being a live flame.

Most of the doctors who were alive at that time have been forgotten.

But the man who felt like a failure is in the history books as the inventor of the box of matches, one of the most successful inventions of modern history.

约翰·沃克尝试着把那些化学品混合起来，观察会发生什么。有一天，一滴非常黏的某种物质粘在了一根棍子的末端，他将它抵在石板上使劲摩擦，想要把那滴物质擦掉。

他没有擦掉那滴物质，却反而使棍子燃烧了起来。

就这样，约翰·沃克发明了世界上第一根简易火柴。只需要用它摩擦粗糙的表面，它立刻就会将一根冰冷干燥的木棍转变为一团真实的火焰。

那个年代的大多数医生现在都被人们遗忘了。

但这位看似失败了的男子，却作为火柴——近代史上最成功的发明之一——的发明者，被永载史册。

---

① **blob** [blɒb] *n.* 一滴、一抹、难以名状的一团
② **match** [mætʃ] 火柴

THE WOMAN TO THANK IF YOU LIKE CHOCOLATE

炼金术士玛丽
巧克力爱好者感谢的女子

MARY HAD A PROBLEM in her **cauldron**①. She was an **alchemist**②.

In movies and books, alchemists are often presented as **wizards**③, but they were often just good chemical scientists, as Mary was.

For her latest experiment to work, she had to take a substance and heat it to a high temperature for a long time. She had to make it melt to produce the **potion**④ she needed.

But every time she tried it, the same thing happened. Just as the melting process began, the edges of the substance would start burning. It quickly ended up as a blackened lump stuck on the bottom of the cauldron. It was so **frustrating**⑤!

How could she solve this problem? There was nobody to ask, because she was one of the first of her kind — this happened a long time ago.

Alchemists should be thought of as very open-minded early scientists. They were interested in physical and chemical reactions, but were also open to **blending**⑥ in a bit of magic if they felt like it.

玛丽是一名炼金术士,但她的坩埚出现了一点问题。

在电影和书籍中,炼金术士通常被当作巫师看待。其实,他们通常是化学方面的优秀科学家,正如玛丽一样。

她最新的一项实验是把某种物质高温加热一定时间,使其熔化,从而提炼出她所需要的药剂。

但每次她尝试做这个实验时,都会发生同一件事:当那种物质开始熔化后,它的边缘就会烧起来,然后全部物质很快烧尽,在坩埚底部留下一团黑色的结块。这真是太令人沮丧了!

她要怎么解决这个问题?她找不到人咨询,因为她是第一个这么做的人——这发生在很久、很久以前。

炼金术士被认为是早期的拥有开放性思维的科学家,他们对物理反应和化学反应都很感兴趣,甚至能接受一些带有魔法色彩的现象。

① **cauldron** [ˈkɔːldr(ə)n; ˈkɒl-] *n.* 大汽锅、大锅,煮皂锅
② **alchemist** [ˈælkɪmɪst] *n.* 炼金术士
③ **wizard** [ˈwɪzəd] *n.* 男巫、术士,奇才;*adj.* 男巫的、巫术的
④ **potion** [ˈpəʊʃ(ə)n] *n.* 一剂、一服,饮剂
⑤ **frustrate** [frʌˈstreɪt] *v.* 使沮丧
⑥ **blend** [blend] *vt.* 混合;*vi.* 混合、协调 [blended 或 blent, blended 或 blent, blending]

If their ancient book said that the experiment worked better if done in the noon sunshine of a mid-summer's day while **chanting** [1] a certain **spell** [2], they would try it that way, and sometimes it did seem to make a difference.

Historians don't know much about Mary except that she was a Jewish woman who lived somewhere in Europe about AD 150.

She was also known as Miriam Prophetissima and Mary the Jewess and was very respected, since she was believed to be the first alchemist in the Western world.

Until she came along, the East had several examples of this type of chemical experimenter, but the West had produced a different sort of scientist (particularly in Greece), who were more philosophical, focused on the principles of physics, mathematics, and other areas.

※※※

So Mary was a pioneer. And she was smart.

She soon worked out that the answer to this problem, as with many science problems, was to find (or in her case, create) the right equipment. She did quite a lot of this. Some historians say she may have invented a **distillation** [3] system and a vapor collection system during her experiments.

But most importantly, it does seem that she solved the puzzle of finding a way to make a fierce heat work in a gentle, consistent way, melting without burning, to turn solids into liquids without turning them into blackened lumps.

如果古籍中记载着，在仲夏正午的阳光下一边念咒语、一边做实验会产生更好的结果，他们就会试着那么做。而有时，那么做似乎真的有用。

历史学家对玛丽的身份所知不多，只知道她是一个在公元 150 年左右生活在欧洲的犹太人。

她也被称为先知玛丽安、犹太女子玛丽，被认为是西方第一位犹太裔炼金术士，人们都非常敬重她。

在她之前，东方已经出现过几位这种类型的化学实验家。但西方的科学家完全不同（尤其是在希腊），他们更具哲理性，致力于研究物理、数学和其他领域的科学原理。

因此，玛丽可以说是一位先驱者，而且还是一位智者。

她很快找到了那项实验所产生问题的解决方案。正如其他很多科学问题一样，解决的方法是需要找到（在她的实验中是"创造"）合适的实验设备。她对此已经轻车熟路了。一些历史学家认为，她很可能在实验过程中发明了蒸馏系统和蒸汽收集系统。

但最重要的是，她采用一种温和而持续的方法形成高温，在不会引起燃烧的情况下将固体熔化成了液体，没有形成黑色结块，由此解决了难题。

① **chant** [tʃɑːnt] *vt.* 唱、颂扬；*vi.* 唱歌、反复地唱歌
② **spell** [spel] 一段时间，魅力
③ **distillation** [ˌdɪstɪˈleɪʃn] *n.* 精馏、蒸馏、净化、蒸馏法、精华、蒸馏物

If you want to understand her problem, you could put some chocolate into a microwave oven. All ovens are different, but most people who do this will find that some parts of the chocolate start to melt, while other parts harden and burn.

To solve the problem, Mary made a two-level cauldron, the bottom one filled with boiling water and the top one containing the substance to be melted.

Water boils always at 100 degrees Celsius, no more. It is not like fire, which can just get hotter and hotter. The two-layer arrangement, with the fire heating the water, and the water heating the thing that needed to be melted, worked perfectly.

The fire could continue to burn, heating the bottom cauldron, but the top cauldron would never go above 100 degrees Celsius.

It caused melting without burning, and spread to alchemists around the world. It became known as a "bain-marie"(which is French for "Mary's bath").

Today, you can find bain-maries in all chemistry labs. But they are even more common in kitchens around the world. That's because you need a bain-marie to melt chocolate, so that you can shape it or use it to coat things, making **yummy**[1] **snacks**[2] and desserts!

The next time you eat anything that is chocolate-covered, spare a thought for Mary, the West's first alchemist, puzzling over her cauldron 18 centuries ago.

如果你想弄明白这个问题，你可以把一些巧克力放进微波炉里。每种微波炉的构造是不同的，但大多数这么做的人会发现：巧克力有一部分开始熔化，然而其余部分则变得更加坚硬并开始燃烧。

玛丽解决这个问题的方法是，她发明了一种双层坩埚，下层装滚烫的开水，上层装需要熔化的物质。

水不像火。火的温度可以变得越来越高，而水在 100 摄氏度沸腾后，就不会再升温。这种双层坩埚就是利用火加热水，再用开水加热需要熔化的物质。真是完美的解决方案！

火持续燃烧，以此来加热底层的坩埚，但上层坩埚的温度永远不会超过 100 摄氏度。

这种加热方式——使物质在不燃烧的情况下熔化——很快在全世界的炼金术士间传播开来，而这种坩埚则被称为"bain-marie"（即法语的"Mary's bath"，字面意思是"玛丽的浴室"，实际意思是"双层蒸锅、水浴"）。

如今，所有的化学实验室中都有这种双层蒸锅。然而它更普遍的日常用途却是用于烹饪，因为它可以熔化巧克力。人们将熔化的巧克力做成各种形状，或用它包裹食材，制作出美味的小吃和甜品。

下一次，在你品尝裹着巧克力外衣的食品时，想一想玛丽吧！她是 1800 年前，西方第一位为坩埚而苦苦思考的炼金术士。

---

① **yummy** [ˈjʌmɪ] *adj.* 好吃的、美味的、令人愉快的；*n.* 美味的东西、令人喜爱的东西 [yummier, yummiest]

② **snack** [snæk] *n.* 小吃、快餐、零嘴（snack 的复数）；*v.* 吃快餐、斗嘴

THE MAN IN THE BURNING HOUSE

加勒特·摩根
着火房屋里的男子

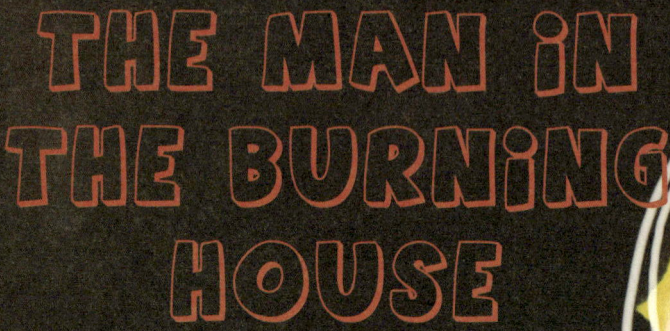

IF SOMETHING NEEDED TO be fixed at the rich man's house, a staff member would call "the **handyman**①".

Except that the handyman wasn't a man at all — he was a dark-skinned boy of 16.

His name was Garrett Augustus Morgan, and he was the son of slaves who married and had children when slavery was **abolished**②.

But though they were not still slaves (this was in the 1890s), they were poor, the boy had little education, and they had to work long hours.

Yet there was one handyman job he really liked: fixing the sewing machine.

Sewing machines were **complicated**③ in those days. You pushed a hanging platform with your feet, and through a bicycle-like system of gears, it made the machine at the top perform its sewing functions.

Garrett became so good at this that when he was in his 20s, he started his own sewing machine repair shop in the American city where he lived.

He realized after a while that when he fixed machines, what he was really doing was the science of engineering — understanding how things are supposed to work and making them work better.

So he became an inventor.

One day he noticed that people who died in house fires usually did not burn to death, but died from **inhaling**④ smoke.

如果富人家里有东西需要修理,管事的会叫来一名"杂务工"。

然而,这名"杂务工"却不是成年人,他只是一个 16 岁的黑人男孩。

他名叫加勒特·奥古斯都·摩根(Garrett Augustus Morgan),他的父母是奴隶,在奴隶制废除时结婚并生下了他。

尽管他们不再是奴隶了(当时是 19 世纪 90 年代),他们还是很穷。加勒特几乎没读过书,他们每天都得工作很长时间。

但有一份杂务工的工作加勒特很喜欢:修理缝纫机。

在那个年代,缝纫机是一种结构复杂的机器。使用者需要用脚踩机器底部悬空的踏板,并通过类似自行车上的齿轮系统的结构带动缝纫机运转。

20 多岁时,加勒特已经对此驾轻就熟了。他在自己的居住地——美国的一座城市——开了一家缝纫机修理店。

不久,他在一次修理机器的过程中意识到,自己正在做的工作其实隶属于工程学范畴——理解物体运行的方式,并让它们更好地运行。

他成了一名发明家。

有一天,加勒特发现,在火灾中遇难的人通常不是被火烧死的,而是因为吸入了太多烟雾而窒息死亡。

---

① **handyman** [ˈhændɪmæn] *n.* 手巧的人、杂务工、水手 [handymen]
② **abolish** [əˈbɒlɪʃ] *vt.* 废除、废止、取消
③ **complicate** [ˈkɒmplɪkeɪt] *vt.* 使复杂化、使恶化 [complicated, complicated, complicating]
④ **inhale** [ɪnˈheɪl] *vt.* 吸入、猛吃猛喝; *vi.* 吸气 [inhaled, inhaled, inhaling]

He knew there was still air in the rooms in which they were trapped. Smoke rises, so there was clear air at floor level.

Garrett Morgan designed a **hood**① with long, **dangling**② tubes. You could move through a smoke-filled room in a burning house and breathe quite well, since the air came from ground level.

But people just didn't believe that a young black man could invent clever, useful things.

So he paid for an actor, who was not black, to pretend to be the inventor. Garrett himself would pretend to be the assistant, and he would don the hood and enter a tent filled with poisonous smoke to **demonstrate**③ how it worked.

One night in 1916 he was fast asleep when a messenger arrived at his house.

There had been an accident in a tunnel deep underground. "Bring your masks," the runner said.

Garrett and his brother rushed to the **scene**④. Workers had been overcome by smoke in a tunnel, and the people who had gone down to **rescue**⑤ them had not come out.

他知道，其实在火灾现场，人们被困的房间里仍有可供呼吸的空气存在。当烟雾上升时，可吸入的新鲜空气沉降在地面附近。

加勒特·摩根设计出了一种带有长长的悬空管子的面罩。当人们需要穿过充满烟雾的火灾现场时，利用这种面罩可以轻松地呼吸到地面附近的新鲜空气。

然而，当时的人们并不相信，像加勒特这样的年轻黑人能够发明出如此巧妙而有用的东西。

因此，加勒特花钱聘请了一位非黑人演员，让他假装是这张面罩的发明者。而加勒特本人则假装是他的一名助手，戴上这张面罩，进入到一个充满了有毒烟雾的帐篷里，亲身示范这张面罩是如何发挥作用的。

✥✥✥

1916年的一个夜晚，加勒特正在熟睡中，一位信使来到他的家中。

地下深处的一条隧道里发生了事故，跑得气喘吁吁的信使说："带上你的面罩。"

加勒特和他的兄弟急忙赶往事故现场。工人们都被烟雾堵在了隧道中，进去救援的人员也没有办法出来。

---

① **hood** [hud] *n*. 风帽、头巾、大学制服后的垂布、(机器等的)罩、(鹰、马的)头罩、(马车等的)车篷、(汽车的)引擎盖

② **dangle** ['dæŋ(ə)l] *vi*. 摇晃地悬挂着；*vt*. 使摇晃地悬挂 [dangled, dangled, dangling]

③ **demonstrate** ['demənstreɪt] *vt*. 证明、展示、论证；*vi*. 示威 [demonstrated, demonstrated, demonstrating]

④ **scene** [siːn] *n*. 场面、情景、景象、事件

⑤ **rescue** ['reskjuː] *vt*. 营救、援救；*n*. 营救、援救、解救 [rescued, rescued, rescuing]

The inventor and his brother used the **masks** to save the rescuers and bring out the bodies of the **victims**②.

Today, people are trained to know that if they are trapped in a burning place, they should put a wet towel around their heads and drop to the ground to breathe the air at floor level.

If you do that, you are kind of creating a Garrett Morgan hood, so say a word of thanks to the handyman who saved lives with it 100 years ago.

加勒特和他的兄弟用发明的面罩救出了救援人员，带出了遇难者的遗体。

如今，人们经过训练得知，当被困在火灾现场时，应该用一条湿毛巾包住自己的头，并卧倒在地，呼吸地面附近的空气。

如果你这么做，你就相当于制作了一个加勒特式面罩。所以，对这位 100 年前用这种面罩拯救了无数生命的杂务工，我们应该心存感激。

① **mask**［mɑːsk］*n.* 面具、口罩
② **victim**［ˈvɪktɪm］*n.* 受害人、牺牲品、牺牲者

THE BOY WHO LOST HIS CHANCE BUT GOT IT BACK

格雷戈里奥·扎拉
机会失而复得的男孩

SOMETIMES YOU GET ONLY one opportunity in life — and someone **snatches**① it away.

That was the sad story for a hard-working boy called Gregorio Zara.

He lived in the town of Lipa in Batangas, the Philippines, and there was not much chance of advancement there.

Except for one thing. There was ONE school prize available. The top performer at high school would get a **scholarship**② to travel to the USA and study there.

It would be just what Gregorio needed. He was a very smart child, but came from a humble family who had no hope of sending him to a fancy university overseas.

Gregorio studied hard all the way through his primary school and high school and succeeded in becoming the top student in the town.

But bad news followed. A high official had demanded that the prize go to a different student.

Gregorio got nothing.

He and his family dealt with the disappointment and he instead went to enroll at a local university.

But some weeks later, there was some surprising news. The person who had taken the scholarship had been taken ill and died.

有时，一个人一生只获得一次机会——却被其他人夺走了。

格雷戈里奥·扎拉（Gregorio Zara），一个勤奋的男孩，就遭遇了这样的悲惨经历。

他住在菲律宾巴坦加斯市的一座名为利帕的小镇上，在那里，他没有太多发展空间。

除了一件事——获得一笔学校奖金。在他所读的那所高中，成绩最好的学生可以获得一笔前往美国深造的奖学金。

这正是格雷戈里奥所需要的。他非常聪明，但家境贫寒，凭自己的经济能力没有机会去国外那些学费昂贵的大学深造。

格雷戈里奥从小学到高中一直努力学习，成功地成为镇上成绩最好的学生。

但坏消息接踵而至。一位高级官员把那份奖学金授予了另一个学生。

格雷戈里奥什么都没有得到。

在他和家人失望之余，格雷戈里奥取而代之，报名去了一所当地的大学。

但几周后，又传来了惊人的消息。那位取代格雷戈里奥获得奖学金的学生生病去世了。

---

① snatch [snætʃ] vt. 夺得、抽空做、及时救助；vi. 抢走 [snatched, snatched, snatching]
② scholarship [ˈskɒləʃɪp] n. 奖学金，学识、学问

Most of the scholarship money had not been spent, and would be given to Gregorio Zara after all. He was going to be an international scholar!

He went to the USA and then to France and quickly became a famous inventor.

He patented many inventions, but one of the most interesting was an early videophone. Way back in 1955, people were still getting used to ordinary telephones, and the idea of a videophone was very **futuristic**①. He called it the "photo phone signal separator network".

But even though Gregorio and other inventors had worked out how to send and receive pictures in phone conversations so long ago, it wasn't until 2006, when many people had computers with the **Skype**② program on them, that video calls became easy, cheap and popular.

Gregorio Zara was a successful scientist and could easily have stayed in the West. But he chose to come back and live in his home country, the Philippines.

He also discovered the law of electrical **kinetic**③ resistance, now called the Zara effect, and created early solar-powered devices. Back home, he married a beauty queen, Engracia Laconico, who was Miss Philippines at one time, and they had four children.

大部分奖学金还没有被动用，格雷戈里奥重新获得了这笔奖学金，成为一名国际交流生！

他先去了美国，随后又前往法国，很快成为一名著名的发明家。

他在很多发明上享有专利，其中最有趣的一项发明是早期的可视电话。在 1955 年，人们还习惯于使用普通的电话，这种可视电话的创意具有极大的前瞻性。格雷戈里奥将其称为"影像电话信号分离器网络"。

不过，即使格雷戈里奥和其他发明家很早就研究出了如何在电话通话中收发照片，但直到 2006 年，当人们开始在电脑上使用网络电话软件时，视频通话才开始变得简便、价廉并流行起来。

格雷戈里奥·扎拉作为一位成功的科学家，本可以轻松自在地居住在西方国家，但他选择了回到家乡菲律宾生活。

他还发现了如今被称为"扎拉效应"的电动阻力定律，并发明了早期的太阳能装置。回到故乡后，他娶了一位名叫拉可妮可（Engracia Laconico）的选美比赛冠军，她曾是一名"菲律宾小姐"。格雷戈里奥与她生了四个孩子。

---

① **futuristic** [fjuːtʃəˈrɪstɪk] *adj.* 未来派的、未来主义的
② **skype** [skaɪp] *n.* 网络电话（一个网络语音沟通工具）
③ **kinetic** [kɪˈnetɪk; kaɪ-] *adj.* [力]运动的、活跃的

Today, when **cartoonists**[①] draw pictures of scientists, they often draw a European man in a white coat with Einstein hair. Actually, Einstein never wore a white coat and stayed away from laboratories!

And if you take a look at history, you find that discoverers, both male and female, came from every culture in the world.

Gregorio Zara died in 1978. If there's such a thing as the afterlife, it would be lovely to have a video-phone conversation with him and see what he thinks of all the Skype-like conversations we have these days!

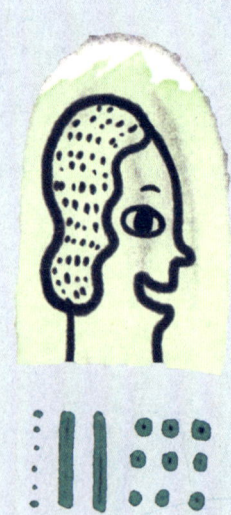

如今，当漫画家描绘科学家的形象时，他们通常会画一个穿着白衣、留着爱因斯坦式爆炸发型的欧洲男人。实际上，爱因斯坦从来没有穿过白色的实验服，而且他不去实验室！

如果你回顾历史，你会发现，作出发明或发现的人——无论男女——可以出自世界上的任何一种文化。

格雷戈里奥·扎拉于1978年逝世。如果有来世，与他进行一场可视通话的话，想必会非常愉快。而且你还可以乘机了解一下，他对于如今所有像网络电话这样的通讯方式有何感想！

① cartoonist [kɑːˈtuːnɪst] n. 漫画家

THE UNLOVED TEENAGER AND THE GIANT CALCULATOR

阿达·拜伦·洛夫莱斯
缺爱少女和大型计算器

ADA WAS A BAD GIRL. And no one was surprised. (As a teenager, she had run off with a man, causing a family **scandal**①.) It was all because of her father, people said — he was famous for being an **immoral**② person.

But the story of this particular teenage girl is worth remembering for several reasons.

First, have you heard of children who are born very rich in terms of money, but very poor in terms of love?

Well, that was Augusta Byron, known as Ada, who was born in the UK in 1815.

She was born into the middle of a **furious**③ argument between her parents, who were always fighting.

Her father was a brilliant man named Lord Byron, who was a wonderful writer but a dreadful husband and father. He treated his wife badly, and had lots of girlfriends, some of whom he also made **pregnant**④.

A month after Ada was born, Lord Byron stormed out of the house, never to return.

Often people can survive without a father, since they at least have mothers — but in Ada's case, her mother was almost as bad as her father.

阿达是一个坏女孩，但没人对此感到惊讶。（十几岁时，她就和一个男人私奔了。这成了他们家的丑闻。）人们说，这都是因为她的父亲——他是出了名的行为不检点的男人。

　　但这位特别的年轻女孩，有很多原因值得被人们所纪念。

　　首先，你有没有听说过这样的孩子，出生于富贵之家，却极度缺少父母的爱？

　　奥古斯塔·拜伦（Augusta Byron）——后来以"阿达"（Ada）的名字广为人知——就是这样的孩子。她于1815年出生在英国。

　　她的父母经常打架，阿达的出生，更成了他们发生冲突的导火索。

　　阿达的父亲拜伦勋爵（Lord Byron）才华横溢，是一位优秀的诗人，但不是一位好丈夫、好父亲。他对妻子很不好，而且交了许多女朋友，其中的一些甚至还怀上了他的孩子。

　　阿达出生一个月后，拜伦勋爵在盛怒之下离家而去，再也没有回来。

　　通常情况下，孩子可以离开父亲生活，因为他们至少还有母亲——但对于阿达来说，她的母亲几乎和父亲一样糟糕。

---

① **scandal** [ˈskænd(ə)l] n. 丑闻、流言蜚语，诽谤、公愤
② **immoral** [ɪˈmɒr(ə)l] adj. 不道德的、邪恶的，淫荡的
③ **furious** [ˈfjʊərɪəs] adj. 激烈的、狂怒的，热烈兴奋的、喧闹的 [more furious，most furious]
④ **pregnant** [ˈpregnənt] adj. 怀孕的

Her mother didn't care much for her own child, leaving her with her grandmother. The woman **pretended**[1] to like occasionally spending time with "it" (that's what she called her child) so that if the marriage was examined in a **divorce**[2] court, she could claim she'd been a good parent.

By the time Ada was 17, she was behaving badly, and ran off to **elope**[3] with her tutor — but her family took her back and hushed up the scandal.

Then, when she was 18, her next tutor (a woman, this time) noticed she was good at mathematics and introduced her to a man named Charles Babbage, who was creating something very strange — a giant calculator.

Ada became his **assistant**[4].

He explained to her how his machine worked. She was very bright and understood it, and she wrote down the process of how the giant calculator worked. (He called it "the Difference Engine", because you pulled a **lever**[5] and it instantly worked out the difference between two numbers.)

Well, if you recognize the name Charles Babbage, you will be able to guess the end of the story.

Charles Babbage is now in the history books as the inventor of the first computer — which was a mechanical device. (Much later, Alan Turing invented the electronic version of the computer.)

阿达的母亲不怎么关心自己唯一的孩子，把阿达丢给她的外祖母照料。这位母亲偶尔会假装很喜欢和"它"相处（她用"它"称呼阿达）。这样即使有一天上法庭离婚，她也可以声称自己是一位好家长。

在17岁时，阿达做出了一个出格的举动——和她的家庭教师私奔了，但不久就被带回了家，丑闻没有传播出去。

18岁时，阿达的第二任家庭教师（一位女士）发现她擅长数学，于是把她推荐给了查尔斯·巴比奇（Charles Babbage），后者发明了一种当时人们十分陌生的东西——大型计算器。

阿达成了查尔斯的助手。

查尔斯向阿达解释他的机器是如何运作的。（查尔斯把它称为"差分机"，因为当你扳动控制杆后，机器会立刻计算出两个数字之间的差异。）阿达非常聪明，理解了原理，并记录下大型计算器运作的过程。

如果你知道查尔斯·巴比奇这个人，你就能猜出故事的结尾了。

查尔斯·巴比奇作为第一台计算机的发明者被载入史册。他发明的这台计算机还只是一种机械装置。[多年之后，阿兰·图灵（Alan Turing）发明了电子计算机。]

① **pretend**［prɪ'tend］*vi.* 假装、伪装、佯装　*vt.* 假装、伪装、模拟
② **divorce**［dɪ'vɔːs］*n.* 离婚、分离；*vt.* 使离婚、使分离、与……离婚；*vi.* 离婚［divorced, divorced, divorcing］
③ **elope**［ɪ'ləʊp］*vi.* 私奔、潜逃［eloped, eloped, eloping］
④ **assistant**［ə'sɪst(ə)nt］*n.* 助手、助理、助教
⑤ **lever**［'liːvə］*n.* 杠杆、控制杆；*vt.* 用杠杆撬动、把……作为杠杆；*vi.* 用杠杆撬

And Ada Lovelace (she became famous under the family name of the man she eventually married) became the world's first computer **programmer**①.

Next time you use a computer, maybe look up and say a word of thanks to the girl, unloved by her father or her mother, who took the one skill she did have and made a difference to history with it.

阿达·洛夫莱斯（Ada Lovelace，她结婚后随夫姓，并以该姓氏而知名）成为世界上第一位计算机程序员。

下次当你使用计算机时，也许可以仰望天空，对这位不被父母所爱的女孩说声谢谢。她利用自己的技能，对历史产生了重要影响。

---

① programmer [ˈprəʊɡræmə] *n.* 程序设计员

THE SCIENTIST AND THE SECRET IN THE ANCIENT BOOK

屠呦呦
发现古籍秘密的科学家

A FATHER THINKING ABOUT a name for his newborn daughter read a line in a poem: "The deer make a you-you sound as they eat the wild hao plants."

The man, whose name was Tu, decided that he liked that sound, and named his bright daughter Youyou.

Tu grew up in the 1930s and 1940s. Little Youyou did well at her school in Ningbo, China, and went on to study **pharmaceuticals**① and Chinese traditional medicine at university. Later, She became an excellent pharmacist.

In the 1960s, China's leader needed at least a few scientists to keep working, because he wanted to find a cure for a killer disease, a type of **malaria**②, which was killing soldiers.

He set up a top-secret department called Project 523. The number came from the date the operation started: May 23, 1967.

So Tu Youyou was **commissioned**③ to find a cure for an incurable strain of a deadly disease.

It seemed an impossible task. By that stage, scientists around the world had tested more than 240,000 compounds and none of them worked.

The global scientific community had failed.

一位父亲正在为他新出生的女儿起名字，他读到一行诗："呦呦鹿鸣，食野之苹。"

这位父亲姓屠，喜欢"呦呦"的鹿鸣声，于是决定给聪明的女儿取名为屠呦呦。

屠呦呦成长于20世纪三四十年代。年幼时的屠呦呦在中国宁波的一所学校读书，成绩优异，进入大学后，她开始研习制药学和中国传统医学，后来成为一名优秀的药学家。

20世纪60年代，中国领导人需要部分科学家继续工作，寻找能够治愈疟疾这种疾病的方法。当时，疟疾是导致士兵大量死亡的主要原因。

于是，一项称为"523计划"的绝密项目开始实施了。523这串数字来自这个项目启动的时间：1967年5月23日。

屠呦呦受命参加，寻找治愈这种致命疾病的疗法。

这看起来像是一项不可能完成的任务。当时，全世界的科学家尝试了24多万种化合物，但无一生效。

全世界的科学家都失败了。

---

① **pharmaceutical** [ˌfɑːməˈsuːtɪk(ə)l; -ˈsjuː-] *adj.* 制药（学）的
② **malaria** [məˈleərɪə] *n.* 疟疾、瘴气
③ **commission** [kəˈmɪʃ(ə)n] *n.* 委员会，佣金，委任，委任状；*vt.* 委任、使服役、委托制作

Tu Youyou, who had come from a book-loving family, had an idea — instead of going to the lab, she went to the library (another thing that the ruling party did not approve of).

She read ancient texts which featured traditional wisdom.

The scientist found a 1,600-year-old book with a curious title: "Emergency **Prescriptions**① to Keep up One's Sleeve". It called for the use of the extract of a Chinese herb called qinghao, or just hao for short.

But she recalled that they had boiled that plant to check its extract, and it hardly worked.

Then, in a paragraph written in AD 340, she read that the essence of the hao plant could not be **extracted**② in hot water.

She tried with aether again and again— and this time it worked, killing the malaria **parasite**③. She needed human volunteers to take it, to prove that it was safe, and she chose herself.

Tu Youyou's medicine worked remarkably well, and has now saved countless lives around the world.

Her achievement was celebrated worldwide when she was given the Nobel Prize.

But when she reflected on her life, she noticed something curious.

出身于书香门第的屠呦呦想出了一个主意——她没有去实验室，而是去了图书馆（这种行为在当时是不允许的）。

屠呦呦阅读古籍，从古人的智慧中寻找方法。

屠呦呦发现，具有 1600 年历史的古代文献《肘后备急方》，倡导使用一种中国草药——青蒿（也可以简称为蒿）的提取物。

但她记得科学家们早就煮过青蒿，试验过它的提取物，但几乎不起作用。

接着，在阅读公元 340 年记录下的一段文字中，屠呦呦发现了一条重要线索：青蒿不能用热水提取。

她一次次地用乙醚进行实验。这一次，提取物生效了，杀死了疟原虫。她还需要通过志愿者试验，确认这种提取物对于人体的安全性。屠呦呦选择了在自己身上进行试验。

屠呦呦提取的药物获得了巨大的成功，至今拯救了全世界不计其数的生命。

她被授予诺贝尔奖，她的成就被全世界所铭记。

在回忆一生时，屠呦呦觉得有一件事很奇妙。

---

① **prescription** [prɪˈskrɪpʃ(ə)n] *n.* 药方、指示、惯例
② **extract** [ˈekstrækt] *vt.* 提取、取出、摘录、榨取；*n.* 汁、摘录、榨出物
③ **parasite** [ˈpærəsaɪt] *n.* 寄生虫、食客

She picked up her father's book of poetry and noticed that his favorite line mentioned the sound that had given her her name, and something else — the wild hao plant that was to be her greatest discovery. "The deer make a you-you sound as they eat the wild hao plants."

Literature really was a remarkable thing.

她翻开父亲抄写的诗集,看到父亲最喜欢的那句"呦呦鹿鸣,食野之苹"。其中的"呦呦"两字成为屠呦呦的名字,而"苹"字指的正是让屠呦呦作出最伟大发现的——青蒿。

文学真是太神奇了!

THE IMPOSSIBLY YOUNG DOCTORS

艾姆巴蒂和矢野祥
令人难以置信的年轻医生

IN THE 1980S, a TV **scriptwriter**[1] thought of a funny idea. When you think of a family doctor at work, you probably think of a wise older person looking after children, right?

But what if the doctor WAS a child?

Some people liked his idea, but others said it couldn't happen. You have to go through years of school before you go to university, and you have to do a long course of medical study before you become a doctor. Most doctors start work at 25 or older.

So the scriptwriter wrote a story in which a child was found to be highly **intelligent**[2] when he was still a toddler, and finished everything early — learning to read and write early, graduating from school early, going to university early, and so on.

The first **episode**[3] of the show, called Doogie Howser, MD, was broadcast as a **comedy**[4] show in the USA in 1989. (The letters MD indicate that a person is a Medical Doctor.)

It was very popular with the public in that country. But what they did not know was that the same things were happening in real life at **roughly**[5] the same time.

A boy called Balamurali Ambati, who was in his early teens, was already at university in New York with the ambition of being a doctor.

二十世纪八十年代，一位电视编剧发现，人们都有一个有趣的想法：当想象一位家庭医生的工作场景时，你想到的多半是一位年长的智者在照看孩子。是不是这样？

但如果这名医生就是一个孩子呢？

有些人喜欢这个主意，但其他人说这是不可能发生的。一个人在上大学前必须经历多年的学习，当上医生前还必须学习很多年的医学课程。大多数医生上岗时的年龄是 25 岁，甚至可能更大一些。

所以这名编剧编撰了一个故事，讲的是一个小孩，还在蹒跚学步时，人们就发现他拥有极高的智商。他做任何事都比常人要早，比如读书、毕业、上大学，等等。

1989 年，喜剧电视剧《天才小医生》在美国开播。（剧名中的"MD"表示主角是一名医生。）

在美国，这部电视剧受到观众的广泛好评。但他们不知道的是，同样的事在现实中也正在发生。

一个名叫巴拉木罗里·艾姆巴蒂（Balamurali Ambati）的男孩，怀揣着成为医生的志向，在十多岁时就进入纽约的一所大学深造。

① **scriptwriter** [ˈskrɪptraɪtə] *n.* 编剧。
② **intelligent** [ɪnˈtelɪdʒ(ə)nt] *adj.* 智能的、聪明的 [more intelligent，most tintelligent]
③ **episode** [ˈepɪsəʊd] *n.* 插曲、一段情节，插话
④ **comedy** [ˈkɒmɪdɪ] *n.* 喜剧、喜剧性，有趣的事情
⑤ **roughly** [ˈrʌflɪ] *adv.* 粗糙地、概略地

And in 1990, when the show was entering its second year, another child was born in the USA who would also be **described**① as a real-life Doogie Howser. His name was Sho Timothy Yano, son of a Japanese father and South Korean mother.

Looking back, we can see that both children followed similar lives to the **fictional**② character. They started reading and writing when they were just toddlers, and went through school at a superfast rate, with their parents doing much of the teaching.

Yano went to university at the age of nine, graduated at 12, and then joined a **prestigious**③ university. But he chose to do a PhD in molecular **genetics**④ and cell biology first, while he was a teenager, and then do a medical degree afterwards. This meant that he was 21 when he became a working doctor.

Balamurali Ambati went straight into medical school at the age of 14, and graduated as a doctor at the age of 17. He told people he was lucky that he was unusually tall (about 6 ft, which is 1.83 m), so people thought he was much older than he was, and he didn't feel out of place.

In 1995, he was listed in the Guinness Book of World Records as the world's youngest doctor, fully qualified by the age of 17.

The lives of both these children teach us something important: these days, even the imaginings of creative screen-writers can become true stories, such are the capabilities of the human race.

在 1990 年，也就是电视剧《天才小医生》播出的第二年，另一个小孩在美国出生了。他也将被描述为现实生活中的天才小医生。他的名字叫矢野祥（Sho Timothy Yano），父亲是日本人，母亲是韩国人。

回顾历史，我们可以看到，这两个孩子都和电视剧中虚拟的人物有着相似的人生。他们都是在蹒跚学步时就开始读书、识字，都以异乎常人的速度完成了学业，他们的父母在两人的教育方面都发挥了巨大作用。

矢野祥 9 岁时读大学，12 岁毕业，接着又进入一所久负盛名的大学，此时他还只是名少年。他选择先攻读分子遗传学和细胞生物学的博士学位，然后再攻读医学。这意味着他年仅 21 岁就成了一名执业医师。

巴拉木罗里·艾姆巴蒂 14 岁时直接进了一所医学院，17 岁毕业，成为一名医生。他对人们说，他很幸运自己有着不同寻常的身高（大约 6 英尺，即 1.83 米），所以人们误以为他比实际年龄大很多。因此他并没有感到自己与别人有什么不同。

1995 年，17 岁的他作为世界上最年轻的医生载入了吉尼斯世界纪录。

这两个孩子的经历告诉我们一些重要的事实：如今，编剧的创造性想象也可以成为现实！人类拥有这样的能力。

---

① **describe** [dɪˈskraɪb] *vt.* 描述、形容、描绘［described，described，describing］
② **fictional** [ˈfɪkʃənl] *adj.* 虚构的、小说的
③ **prestigious** [preˈstɪdʒəs] *adj.* 有名望的、享有声望的
④ **genetics** [dʒɪˈnetɪks] *n.* 遗传学

THE MOTHERLESS CHILD WHO SOLVED HIS FATHER'S PROBLEM

布莱斯·帕斯卡
帮助父亲解决难题的失恃男孩

WHEN A YOUNG MOTHER died of illness, people felt sorry for her three little children, Gilberte, Blaise and Jacqueline.

What would happen to them?

Fortunately, the three children were looked after by their father, a **judge**①, and his servants.

The judge decided that his children were unusually clever. Probably most parents think so about their children, but the judge actually did something about it — he decided that he himself would be their teacher, and they would all be home-schooled by him.

Blaise, who had been just three years old when his mother died, soon showed that he was extremely good with science and mathematics.

By the time he was a teenager, Blaise Pascal was writing scientific papers, just like a university professor.

At the age of 16, he wrote a paper about something called the **Mystic**② **Hexagram**③, which was a mathematical problem that had puzzled experts for years.

But then the family's luck turned bad again.

His father lost his job as a judge, and the family became very poor.

The man of the house eventually got a job as a tax collector, so they had some income. Yet the work was really hard, and the former judge asked his son Blaise to help him sort through thousands and thousands of sheets of numbers **scribbled**④ on paper.

一位母亲年纪轻轻就被疾病夺去了生命，撇下三个孩子——吉尔伯特、布莱斯和杰奎琳。人们都为他们感到难过。

这三个孩子会怎么样呢？

幸运的是，他们的法官父亲和仆人把他们照料得很好。

这位法官发现他的孩子异常聪明，可能大多数父母都会觉得自己的孩子比别人家的聪明。法官父亲准备为孩子们做点什么：他决定亲自教三个孩子，让他们在家里接受教育。

❦❦❦

母亲去世时，布莱斯年仅三岁，但他很快展现出了自己在科学和数学方面的天赋。

十几岁时，布莱斯·帕斯卡（Blaise Pascal）就像大学教授一样，开始撰写科学论文。

16岁时，他写了一篇关于神秘的六角星形的论文。这个数学难题已经困惑专家许多年了。

但接着，这个家庭的运气又开始变差了。

他们的法官父亲失去了工作，整个家庭一贫如洗。

父亲最终得到了一份收税员的工作，家庭有了一些收入。然而这份工作非常辛苦，这位前法官让儿子布莱斯帮忙，将纸上成千上万个书写潦草的数据进行排序。

---

① **judge** ［dʒʌdʒ］ *vt.* 判断、审判；*n.* 法官、裁判员；*vi.* 审判、判决［judged, judged, judging］

② **mystic** ［'mɪstɪk］ *adj.* 神秘的、神秘主义的；*n.* 神秘主义者

③ **hexagram** ［'heksəɡræm］ *n.* 六线形、六角星形

④ **scribble** ［'skrɪb(ə)l］ *n.* 潦草写成的东西、潦草的写法、杂文；*vt.* 乱写、潦草地书写；*vi.* 乱写、乱涂［scribbled, scribbled, scribbling］

Now all this happened a long time ago, in the 1600s in France, long before there were computers or calculators. That meant it was a difficult job to be a tax collector. Every **sum**① had to be added up using pencil and paper, and it was really important that not one number was wrong.

Blaise found the job just as tough as his father did.

But the child was creative. He realized that because numbers were logical, he should be able to build a machine that could **process**② them, using a system of levers. You probably know what an **abacus**③ is. The device he designed was a bit like a small, automatic abacus, inside a box.

So, at the age of 16, he started to work on a **portable**④ calculating machine. Of course, these were not electric ones like we have — electricity had not really been discovered then, not for general use, anyway.

By the time he was 18, he had created a mechanical calculator that could add and **subtract**⑤, and which gave the right answer every time. The machine was called Pascal's calculator or the Pascaline — and he became famous.

这一切发生在 17 世纪的法国，那时没有计算器，也没有计算机。这意味着收税员是一份艰辛的工作，每一笔金额都必须用纸和笔来计算累加，而且极其重要的是，不能有任何错误。

布莱斯发现帮忙做的这件事和父亲所做的工作一样困难。

但这个男孩有着创造性的思维，他意识到，数字之间是有逻辑关系的，他应该可以发明一种机器，利用杠杆系统处理这些数字。你可能知道算盘，布莱斯设计的就是一种位于盒子内部、类似于小型自动化算盘的装置。

从此以后，16 岁的布莱斯开始用这种便携式的计算器工作。当然，那并不是我们如今使用的电子计算器。当时电还没在真正意义上被发明出来，至少还没有普遍使用。

18 岁时，布莱斯发明了一种机械化的计算器，可以进行加减运算，而且从未出错。这个机器被称为帕斯卡计算器或是帕斯卡加法器。帕斯卡出名了。

① **sum**［sʌm］*n*. 金额、总数；*vi*. 概括；*vt*. 总结、合计［summed, summed, summing］
② **process**［prə'ses; (n.)'prəʊses］*vt*. 处理、加工；*n*. 过程、进行、方法、步骤、作用、程序，推移；*vi*. 列队前进［processes, processed, processed, processing］
③ **abacus**［'æbəkəs］*n*. 算盘［abacuses 或 abaci］
④ **portable**［'pɔːtəb(ə)l］*adj*. 手提的、便携式的、轻便的
⑤ **subtract**［səb'trækt］*vt*. 减去、扣掉

A few of his original calculators still exist, and you can see them in museums in Paris and in Dresden, Germany.

But the next time you use your calculator to do mathematics at school, spare a thought for the motherless son who created the first calculator, to help the father he loved.

Blaise Pascal grew up to become a famous scientist, mathematician, and Christian philosopher.

He said lots of interesting things that people are still discussing today, such as this: "The supreme function of reason is to show man that some things are beyond reason."

如今，你可以在德国德累斯顿和法国巴黎的博物馆中看到尚存于世的一些帕斯卡计算器的原件。

当你下次在学校里用计算器进行数学运算时，想想这位失去了母亲、为了帮助他敬爱的父亲而创造了第一个计算器的孩子吧！

布莱斯·帕斯卡长大后，成了著名的科学家、数学家和信奉基督教的哲学家。

他说过很多有趣的话，人们至今还津津乐道，比如这句："理性至高无上的作用是向人们展示，有些事物是超越理性的。"

THE GIRL TORN BETWEEN TWO CAREERS

蕾切尔·卡森
在两种职业之间摇摆的女孩

TEENAGER RACHEL CARSON WAS PUZZLED. Most young people have no idea what they want to do when they grow up — but she had the opposite problem.

There were TWO things she really wanted to do. And she couldn't choose between them.

Rachel was born in 1907 on a farm in the United States and **absolutely**① loved nature. So it seemed like she was destined to be a scientist.

But she loved reading novels, and her short stories had been published in a magazine. So it seemed like she was destined to be a writer.

Which was it to be? Scientist? Or writer? Rachel, who was a Christian, **wrestled**② with the problem. Why had God given her such a **challenge**③?

She was still **confused**④ when she applied to college. Rachel **enrolled**⑤ as an English student, so that she could study literature, and then decided she had made a mistake. She switched courses, starting again as a science student.

一个名叫蕾切尔·卡森（Rachel Carson）的年轻人很烦恼。大多数年轻人对于长大后想要从事的职业一无所知——但她恰恰有着相反的困惑。

她想要从事的职业有两种，她不知道该如何抉择。

❧❧❧ ❦❦❦

蕾切尔1907年出生在美国的一个农场中。她非常喜爱大自然，似乎命中注定，她长大后会成为一位科学家。

但她也爱读小说，而且她写的短篇小说曾刊登在一本杂志上，似乎命中注定，她长大后会成为一位作家。

那么到底做什么呢？科学家还是作家？蕾切尔是一位基督徒，她一直被这个问题所困扰：为什么上帝要让她面对这个难题呢？

❧❧❧ ❦❦❦

申请大学时，蕾切尔仍然被这个问题困扰着。她是作为英语系学生注册入学的，所以她可以学习文学。但她很快发现自己的决定是错误的，于是换了课程，作为科学系学生重新开始学习。

---

① **absolutely** [ˈæbsəluːtlɪ] *adv.* 绝对地、完全地
② **wrestle** [ˈres(ə)l] *n.* 摔跤、搏斗、斗争；*vi.* 摔跤、斗争、斟酌；*vt.* 与摔跤、与……搏斗、使劲搬动 [wrestled, wrestled, wrestling]
③ **challenge** [ˈtʃælɪn(d)ʒ] *n.* 挑战、怀疑；*vt.* 向……挑战、对……质疑
④ **confuse** [kənˈfjuːz] *vt.* 使混乱、使困惑。[confused, confused, confusing]
⑤ **enroll** [ɪnˈrəʊl] *vt.* 登记、使加入、把……记入名册、使入伍；*vi.* 参加、登记、注册、记入名册

It was frustrating.

But she didn't have time to worry about this puzzle.

Her family was very poor, and several members were suddenly struck by illness.

So that meant that after she finished college, she had to take whatever jobs she could find, to earn money to feed her troubled family.

Her life was quite difficult for a long time. But finally, after years of struggling, everything started to **click into place**[①].

Science is important, but very hard to explain — and the special skill of good writers is that they are great at explaining things. THAT was where she would fit in.

She realized that when she had switched from studying writing to studying science, all she was really doing was giving herself, a writer at heart, something important to write about.

Rachel also realized that the books she had read when she was young were great stories — but all had a nature **theme**[②]. As a little girl, she loved Peter Rabbit, and as she became a teenager, she had read Moby-Dick, the story of a man trying to find a great whale.

※※※

Well, you may be able to guess the next part of Rachel Carson's story. Yes, she became a science writer. And in 1962, when she was 54 years old, she wrote a book called "Silent Spring", and that made her famous. It was a book about the harm that **pesticides**[③] were doing to the environment. She died in 1964.

多么令人沮丧啊!

但蕾切尔没有时间为此发愁。她的家庭非常贫穷,而且好几位家庭成员突然病倒了。

所以,这意味着蕾切尔一读完大学就必须立刻去赚钱。无论做什么工作,只要能挣钱养活家人就行。

她经历了一段艰难的岁月。但经过多年的奋斗之后,一切都开始步入正轨。

科学很重要,但很难解释。优秀作家的过人之处就是他们擅长解释。这种工作蕾切尔非常胜任。

蕾切尔意识到,当学习的专业从写作改为科学后,她所做的一切都是为自己提供写作的重要素材。

蕾切尔同时也意识到,自己小时候读过的那些精彩故事,都与大自然这个主题有关。小时候她喜欢比得兔;而在青少年时期,她阅读过《白鲸》,这本书讲述一个男人寻找白鲸的故事。

好了,你大概可以猜出蕾切尔·卡森接下来的经历了。是的,她成了一名科学作家。1962 年,在她 54 岁时,她的成名作《寂静的春天》出版,该书讲述杀虫剂对环境的危害。蕾切尔于 1964 年去世。

---

① **click into place**:(比喻)突然明了,变得清楚,(机械装置)正好嵌入,水落石出,恰好吻合。
② **theme** [θi:m] *n.* 主题、主旋律、题目
③ **pesticide** [ˈpestɪsaɪd] *n.* 杀虫剂

But that wasn't the end of the story. Her message **inspired**[1] the setting up of the **US Environmental Protection Agency**[2].

Today, most people know that humans are damaging the environment, and historians list Rachel Carson as one of the founders of the green movement.

但这并不是故事的结局。她在著作中描绘的环境状况，促使美国成立环境保护局。

如今，世界上的大多数人都明白，人类正在破坏自然环境。而历史学家则把蕾切尔·卡森列为绿色运动的创始者之一。

① inspire ［ɪn'spaɪə］ vt. 激发、鼓舞、启示、使产生灵感［inspired, inspired, inspiring］
② US Environmental Protection Agency 美国环境保护局

The Young Scientists Series:
The Inventor's Spark and Breakers of Barriers

by

Nury Vittachi

English Copyright © 2017 by World Scientific Publishing Co. Pte. Ltd.

Bi-lingual (Simplified Chinese & English) Character Copyright © 2018 by Shanghai Scientific & Technological Education Publishing House

Shanghai Scientific & Technological Education Publishing House published bi-lingual edition by arranged with World Scientific Publishing Co. Pte. Ltd., Singapore

All rights reserved. This book, or parts thereof, may not be reproduced in any form or by any means, electronic or mechanical, including photocopying, recording or any information storage and retrieval system now known or to be invented, without written permission from the Publisher.

ALL RIGHTS RESERVED
上海科技教育出版社业经World Scientific Publishing Co. Pte. Ltd.同意取得本书中英文双语版版权

责任编辑	侯慧菊
封面设计	杨　静

"伟人的少年故事"丛书
创新的火花——打破隔阂创造历史的伟人
［斯里兰卡］努雷·维塔奇（Nury Vittachi）　著
斯泰帕·张（Step Cheung）　图
朱之翀　译
张　群　审校

出版发行	上海科技教育出版社有限公司
	（上海市柳州路218号　邮政编码200235）
网　址	www.ewen.co　www.sste.com
经　销	各地新华书店
印　刷	上海昌鑫龙印务有限公司
开　本	889×1194　1/32
印　张	3
版　次	2018年8月第1版
印　次	2018年8月第1次印刷
书　号	ISBN 978-7-5428-6703-2/G·3829
图　字	09-2017-937号
定　价	25.00元

扫描二维码
获取教师参考资料
及练习答案

扫描二维码
获取学生练习册